BOLD KIDS

MW01139857

Colorado

CHILDREN'S AMERICAN LOCAL HISTORY BOOK WITH FACTS!

This list of facts about Colorado for kids will help them learn about the state's geography. The state is part of the Mountain States and is the 38th state in the U.S. Constitution.

The quick reference guide will make it easy for your kids to learn about the state in no time at all. If you need to study fast for an upcoming test, this is the perfect tool.

One of the most fascinating facts about Colorado is that it is home to the highest average elevation of all US states. The Rocky Mountains cover much of the west side of the state, from New Mexico all the way to Canada.

Mount Elbert is the state's highest peak. A large red C filled with gold and a white background are the state symbols. Eagles are also popular in the state, as they are federally protected. Other fun facts about Colorado for kids include things like the state flower, giant forks, and burgers.

The state flower is the blue columbine, which is illegal to pick in Colorado. The state's symbols are a large red C filled with gold, a blue and white background, and an eagle.

The eagle is the state's official bird of prey, so it's illegal to harm them. Besides eagles, the state celebrates Mike The Headless Chicken Day on 10 September.

In addition to being the fourth highest state in the U.S., Colorado is known for its mountainous terrain. Its western side is dominated by the Rocky Mountains, which stretch from New Mexico to Canada. The state's tallest peak, Mount Elbert, is located in the highlands.

Its northern border is characterized by the Great Plains, a vast grassland that covers much of North America. The largest mountain is Mount Elbert, which is the tallest peak in the Rocky Mountains. Among the many weird facts about Colorado for kids, the most intriguing are those about beer and burgers.

Among the many weird and interesting facts about Colorado are its native people. While this state has many Native American tribes, it is also home to two large reservations of Native Americans. The state's two Indian casinos are located outside of the main three casino towns in the state.

Although the locals call themselves "natives" in Colorado, they call themselves "colorado" and are proud of their heritage. There are even some bizarre facts about the U.S.'s capital city, Denver.

Among the state's many symbols, Colorado has a variety of colorful flowers. The blue columbine is its state flower, which has been banned since 1925. Several eagles can be seen in the state's logo, which is a large red C surrounded by a blue and white background.

The colorful rocks and burgers of Colorado are popular with visitors, so it's no wonder the state is a popular destination for vacations.

The state's red rocks and national landmarks have made it an iconic state in the United States. The colorful rock formations of the Rocky Mountains are also its signature feature.

A Colorado souvenir is a piece of art, and you'll probably be able to find it in the surrounding area. Whether you're looking for a piece of art or an original painting, you'll find the most fascinating facts about Colorado.

The state's red and white color makes it a diverse place for people. For example, the blue columbine is the state flower, but picking it is illegal. In 1858, a gold mine was discovered in the city of Denver.

The city of Denver is also the home of the world's first rodeo. In fact, the State is the only U.S. state to decline to host the Olympic games.

The state flower is the blue columbine, and it is illegal to pick this flower in the state. The state's red stones are considered a symbol of Colorado. These colors also symbolize its diverse history. The blue and white background of the Colorado flag symbolizes the state's beauty.

The big red C in the logo of the State Capitol building is a symbol of the nation, as it represents its high altitude mountains. In addition to mountains, the state is home to giant forks and burgers.

CPSIA information can be obtained
at www.ICGtesting.com
Printed in the USA
LVHW072224110723
752229LV00042B/1531